# Chill with
# Chopin

9 tranquil masterpieces for piano

# Chill with
# Chopin

## CD track listing

1. **Berceuse in D flat major, Op.57**  (5:23)
   Silvia Cápová (piano), Slovak RSO (Bratislava), Peter Breiner

2. **Nocturne in D flat major, Op.27 No.2**  (6:14)
   Idil Biret (piano)

3. **Impromptu in F sharp major, Op.36**  (5:45)
   Idil Biret (piano)

4. **Nocturne in C sharp minor, BI 49 (arr. Piatigorsky)**  (3:45)
   Maria Kliegel (cello), Bernd Glemser (piano)

5. **Nocturne in B flat minor, Op.9 No.1**  (5.35)
   Idil Biret (piano)

6. **Piano Concerto No.2: Larghetto**  (9:25)
   Idil Biret (piano), Slovak State Philharmonic, Robert Stankovsky

7. **Nocturne in E minor, Op.72 No.1 (posth.)**  (4:37)
   Idil Biret (piano)

8. **Prelude in D flat major, Op.28 No.15 'Raindrop'**  (5:49)
   Idil Biret (piano)

9. **Mazurka No.13 in A minor, Op.17 No.4**  (4:35)
   Idil Biret (piano)

10. **Andante spianato in G and Grande Polonaise in G Op.22: Allegro maestoso**  (4:47)
    Idil Biret (piano)

11. **Sonata for Cello and Piano in G minor, Op.65: Largo**  (3:25)
    Maria Kliegel (cello), Bernd Glemser (piano)

12. **Grande Valse brillante in A minor, Op.34 No.2**  (5:30)
    Idil Biret (piano)

13. **Piano Concerto No.1: Romanza – Larghetto**  (11:43)
    Idil Biret (piano), Slovak State Philharmonic, Robert Stankovsky

© 2006 by Faber Music Ltd
First published in 2006 by Faber Music Ltd
Bloomsbury House
74–77 Great Russell Street
London WC1B 3DA
Printed in England by Caligraving Ltd
Photography: www.richardduckett.com
All rights reserved.

ISBN10: 0-571-52438-9
EAN13: 978-0-571-52438-9

To buy Faber Music publications or to find out about the full range of titles available
please contact your local music retailer or Faber Music sales enquiries.

Faber Music Limited, Burnt Mill, Elizabeth Way, Harlow, CM20 2HX England
Tel: +44 (0)1279 82 89 82   Fax: +44 (0)1279 82 89 83
sales@fabermusic.com   fabermusic.com

# Introduction

Born near Warsaw in 1810, the son of a French émigré and a Polish mother, Fryderyk Chopin was a prodigiously gifted child. He entered the Warsaw Conservatory at the age of sixteen and left three years later with a report from the head of the conservatory that read 'Lessons in musical composition: Chopin, F., third year student, amazing capabilities, a musical genius'. It is for his myriad solo piano works that he is far and away best known: as a pianist himself he instinctively knew how best to write for that instrument and in fact did not write a single work that did not include a piano in some capacity.

Of all the various genres in which Chopin wrote, it is perhaps the nocturnes ('night pieces') that best sum up what his style was all about. Though he was not the first composer to write in this genre, he took the existing form and moulded it into something unmistakeably his own. Another form with which Chopin is often accredited as having brought to fruition is the mazurka, though it was already a popular dance in the fashionable ballrooms of western Europe by the time he arrived in Paris. This sometimes contemplative, sometimes vigorous traditional Polish dance in 3 time is similar to the waltz, but distinguished from it by the accenting of the weak beats of the bar.

'Listening to beautiful music is one of life's great pleasures, and there's certainly no better way to relax than to the sound of dreamy works by a composer like Chopin. But after you've listened, what better than to actually get to grips with the music yourself? I know that the piano music in this book – music that reflects the chill out mood of the CD – is exactly the kind I've enjoyed playing all my life. Gorgeous pieces you can really lose yourself in; some quite challenging but none too fiendishly difficult to master. A wonderful way to chill out – and extend your repertoire while you're at it.'

Katie Derham
*Classic FM presenter and ITV news presenter*

# Prelude in A major

## Op.28 No.7

# Prelude in E minor

## Op.28 No.4

# Mazurka in A minor

## Op.17 No.4

# Nocturne in G minor

Op.37 No.1

# Mazurka in C major

## Op.67 No.3

# Prelude in D flat major 'Raindrop'

## Op.28 No.15

# Nocturne in E minor

## Op.72 No.1

# Waltz in A flat major 'L'adieu'

## Op.69 No.1

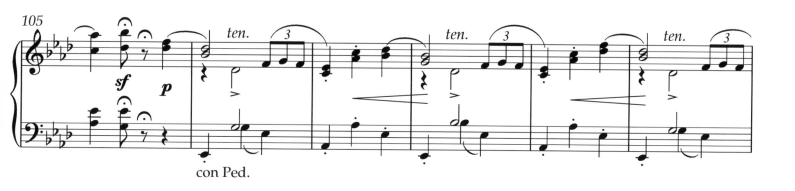

# Marche Funèbre

*from* Sonata in B flat minor

# For more in a chilled mood
# try the rest of the series ...
# each with a free Naxos CD

### Adagio Chillout
Favourite slow movements and contemplative pieces,
including Beethoven's *Moonlight Sonata*,
Schumann's *Träumerei* and Mendelssohn's
*Song without words 'Sweet Remembrance'*.

0-571-52435-4

### Chill with Chopin
Including masterpieces such as the *'Raindrop'* Prelude,
the *March Funèbre* from Sonata in B flat minor, and
the Waltz in A flat *'L'Adieu'*.

0-571-52438-9

### Chill with Mozart
The most beautiful movements by Mozart,
including the first movement from Sonata in C K.545,
the Fantasia in D minor K.397 and
Adagio in B minor K.540.

0-571-52436-2

### Chill with Debussy
Unmissable favourites such as *Clair de lune*,
*La fille aux cheveux de lin* and *Arabesque* No.1.

0-571-52437-0